UNIT 4 BOOK 2

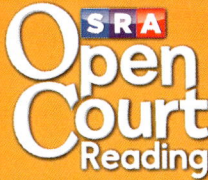

# Light and Sound

Grade 1

## Program Authors

Carl Bereiter, Ph.D.
Andrew Biemiller, Ph.D.
Joe Campione, Ph.D.
Doug Fuchs, Ph.D.
Lynn Fuchs, Ph.D.

Steve Graham, Ph.D.
Karen Harris, Ph.D.
Jan Hirshberg, Ed.D.
Anne McKeough, Ph.D.
Marsha Roit, Ed.D.

Marlene Scardamalia, Ph.D.
Marcy Stein, Ph.D.
Gerald H. Treadway Jr, Ph.D.

## Photo Credits

**52** Rob Friedman/Getty Images. **Back Cover:** rozbyshaka/iStock/Getty Images Plus, Jodie Griggs/Moment Open/Getty Images, ©KidStock/Blend Images LLC.

## Acknowledgments

Grateful acknowledgment is given to the following publishers and copyright owners for permissions granted to reprint selections from their publications. All possible care has been taken to trace ownership and secure permission for each selection included. In case of any errors or omissions, the Publisher will be pleased to make suitable acknowledgments in future editions.

"Flicker, Flash, Ka-boom!" by Valerie Marchini and art by Maribel Suarez; Ladybug Magazine, April 2013. Copyright © by Carus Publishing Company. Reproduced with permission. All Cricket Media material is copyrighted by Carus Publishing Company, d/b/a Cricket Media, and/or various authors and illustrators. Any commercial use or distribution of material without permission is strictly prohibited. Please visit http://www.cricketmedia.com/info/licensing2 for licensing and http://www.cricketmedia.com for subscriptions.

Just Listen by Kathleen Weidner; Click Magazine, July 2013. Copyright © by Carus Publishing Company. Reproduced with permission. All Cricket Media material is copyrighted by Carus Publishing Company, d/b/a Cricket Media, and/or various authors and illustrators. Any commercial use or distribution of material without permission is strictly prohibited. Please visit http://www.cricketmedia.com/info/licensing2 for licensing and http://www.cricketmedia.com for subscriptions.

"Onomatopoeia" from IT DOESN'T ALWAYS HAVE TO RHYME by Eve Merriam. Copyright ©1964, 1992 by Eve Merriam. "Weather" from CATCH A LITTLE RHYME by Eve Merriam. Copyright ©1966, 1994 Eve Merriam. Both are reprinted by permission of Marian Reiner.

# MHEonline.com

Copyright © 2016 McGraw-Hill Education

All rights reserved. No part of this publication may be reproduced or distributed in any form or by any means, or stored in a database or retrieval system, without the prior written consent of McGraw-Hill Education, including, but not limited to, network storage or transmission, or broadcast for distance learning.

Send all inquiries to:
McGraw-Hill Education
8787 Orion Place
Columbus, OH 43240

ISBN: 978-0-07-669427-3
MHID: 0-07-669427-5

Printed in the United States of America.

6 7 8 9 MER 25 24 23

# UNIT 4 Light and Sound

Book 2

## Table of Contents

**Flicker, Flash, Ka-boom!** . . . . . . . . . . . . . . . . . . . . . . 4
   by Valerie Marchini
   illustrated by Maribel Suarez

**Just Listen** . . . . . . . . . . . . . . . . . . . . . . . . . . . . . . . . 6
   by Kathleen Weidner Zoehfeld
   illustrated by Dave Kirwan

**The Tale of Lightning and Thunder** . . . . . . . . . . . 30
   by Edwin Clark
   illustrated by Olivia Chin Mueller

**Weather** . . . . . . . . . . . . . . . . . . . . . . . . . . . . . . . . . 48
   by Eve Merriam
   illustrated by Stephanie Dehennin

**Onomatopoeia** . . . . . . . . . . . . . . . . . . . . . . . . . . . 50
   by Eve Merriam
   illustrated by Stephanie Dehennin

**Glossary** . . . . . . . . . . . . . . . . . . . . . . . . . . . . . . . . 52

**Essential Questions** What types of sounds have you heard during a thunderstorm? How did they make you feel?

# Flicker, Flash, Ka-boom!

by Valerie Marchini
illustrated by Maribel Suarez

I am brave
My dog is not.
Raindrops fall faster
*Plip plop! Plip plop!*

Flicker and flash
Then loud *ka-booms!*
Ready to hide
He runs through rooms

Behind the couch
Under the chairs
Not a good place
He runs up the stairs

He wants to hide
His body and head.
You'll find him here
Tucked under my bed!

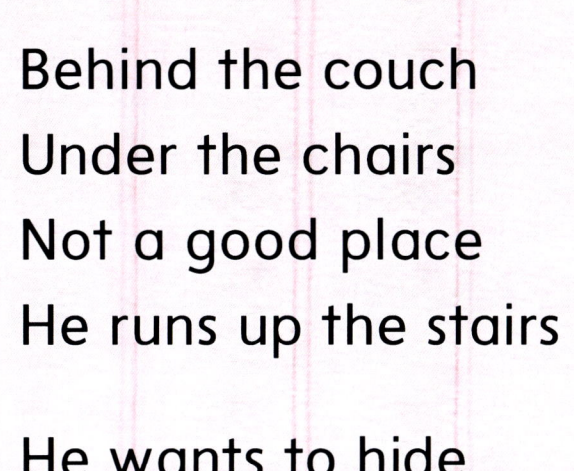

**Essential Questions** What sounds do you hear outside? What sounds do you hear inside?

# Just Listen

*by Kathleen Weidner Zoehfeld*
*illustrated by Dave Kirwan*

*Psssst*! Your friend leans close and whispers a secret. *Woof*! *Woof*! His dog barks as a car zooms past.

*Beep beep*! The driver honks her horn to say hello. People and animals and things are making sounds all the time.

But what is sound?

And how do we hear it?

Pluck a guitar string or a rubber band stretched between your fingers. You see the string or rubber band go back and forth very fast. It is vibrating.

You can't see it, but the vibration makes waves in the air, like you make waves in a bathtub of water when you waggle your hand up and down quickly.

Every sound is made by vibrations. Place your fingertips lightly on the front of your throat. Say or shout a few words. Feel the tiny, quick, shaking movements?

I can feel it!

That is the vibration of the vocal cords in your throat. It makes the sound of your voice.

When you say "hello," your vocal cords vibrate, sending sound waves through the air.

Hello!

Your ears are sound wave collectors. Sit very quietly. Listen to all the different sounds you can hear.

The sound waves your ear collects travel through your ear canal. At the end of the canal is a thin piece of skin called an eardrum. The sound waves make your eardrum vibrate.

Special nerve hairs farther inside your ear pick up the vibrations. They send signals to your brain. Your brain makes sense of all the sounds you hear.

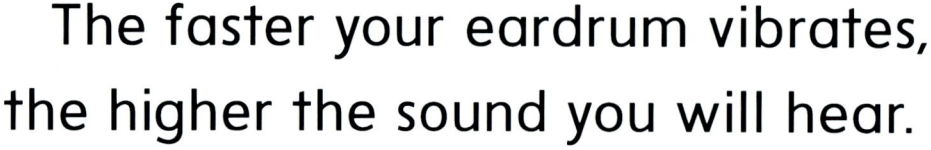

Sound waves travel not only through air but through water. They can even travel through solid things, like wood.

Knock on your table top.
Listen to the sound.

Does the knock sound different?

Now put one ear down on your table and knock again the same way.

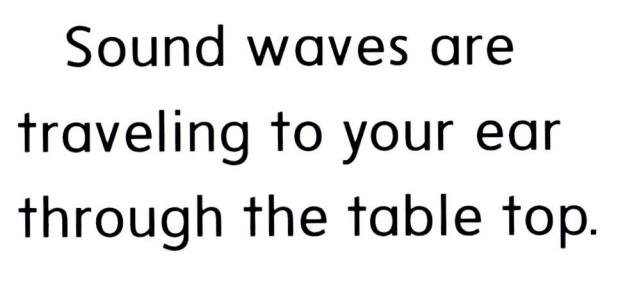

In outer space, there is no air. And guess what? There are no sounds, either, because there is nothing for sound waves to travel through. If an astronaut bangs a hammer on the outside of a spaceship, people inside the spaceship might hear it.

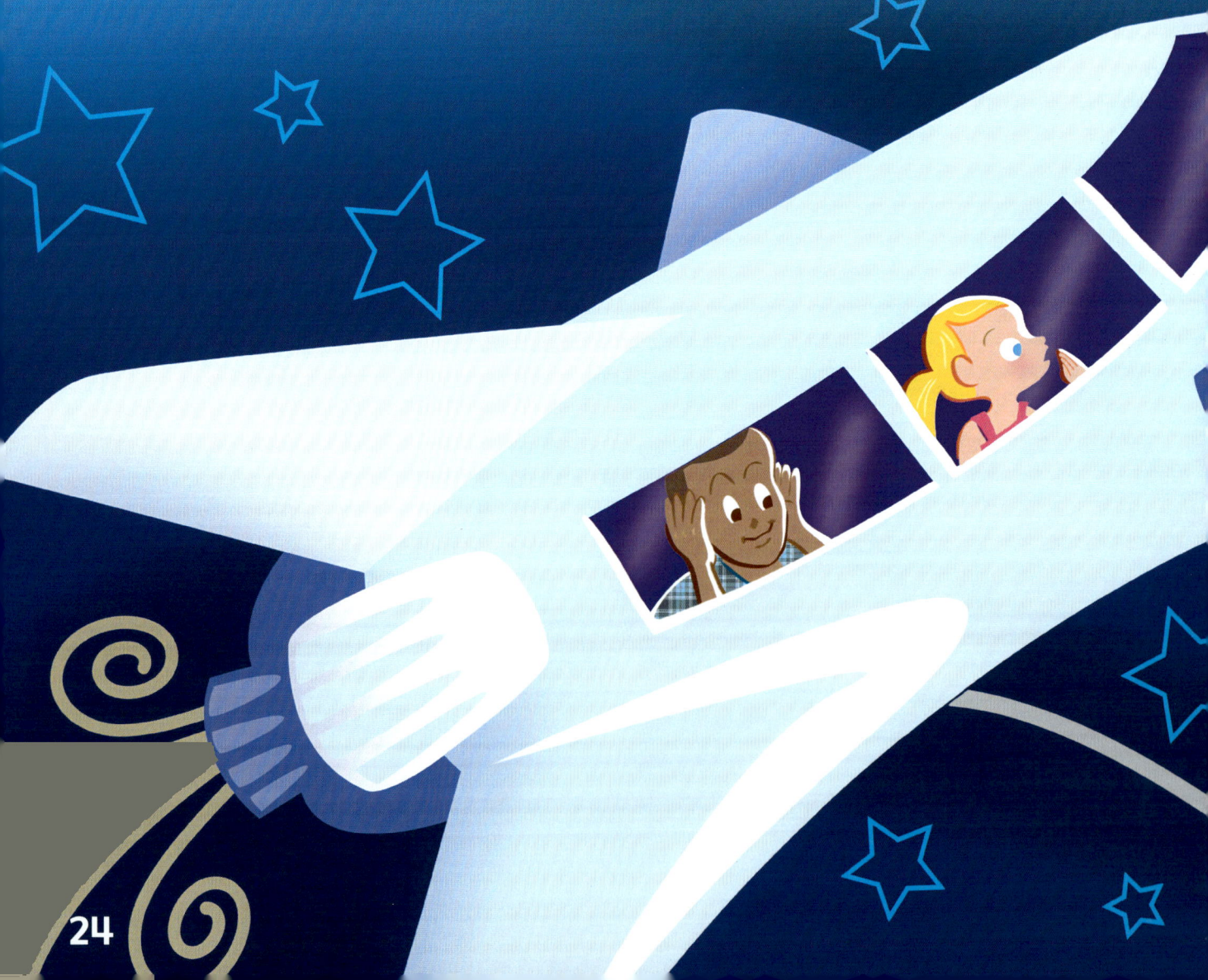

But there will be no sound outside the ship—no matter how hard the astronaut hammers! Because there is no air, the hammering creates no sound waves. There is only silence.

I don't hear anything.

Sometimes your ear collects a sound twice. If you make a wave with water in the tub it will go to the edge and bounce back. Sometimes sound waves bounce back too.

If you clap your hands in an empty room, you hear the clap as soon as your hands come together.

But you may hear it again, a split second later, as the sound waves travel to the wall and bounce back to your ear.

It's called an echo.

The world is full of sounds.
Just listen.

What do you hear?

**Essential Question** How does this author use his imagination to describe lightning and thunder?

# The Tale of Lightning & Thunder

by Edwin Clark
illustrated by Olivia Chin Mueller

Long ago, there lived a brother and sister. The girl's name was Eliora. The boy's name was Samuel. Eliora and Samuel were twins.

Eliora and Samuel lived in a giant castle in the clouds. The twins enjoyed rolling and tumbling way up in the sky.

Eliora had a friendly smile. Mother called her smile a ray of sunshine. Samuel had a contagious laugh. Mother said his laugh rumbled like a drum.

Eliora and Samuel loved living in their castle. However, they did not like it when fierce storms blew in and forced them to stay inside.

The howling wind and pounding rain scared the twins. Sometimes the clouds turned black with rain. Then the twins hid under mounds of blankets.

One day, a scary storm blew in. Rain lashed at the castle windows. The wind made the walls tremble and shake.

Eliora and Samuel ran into their bedroom. They hid under the blankets on their beds. They wanted the storm to go away.

Mother and Father knew the twins were afraid of the storm. So they knocked on their bedroom door. "Can we come in?" they asked.

Eliora and Samuel peeked out from under the blankets. "Can you make the storm go away?" they asked.

"No, we cannot," Mother said. "But I can tell you a story. It will make you forget about the storm."

Eliora and Samuel crawled out from under the blankets. They snuggled close to hear Mother's story.

Mother told them a funny story. As they listened to Mother's story, the twins started to forget about the storm.

Soon, Eliora was smiling again. A flash of light lit the room. Soon Samuel was laughing again. His laughter rumbled like a drum.

When Mother's story finished, Father began to tell his tale. Story after story, the twins began to feel braver. Eliora smiled more. The flash of light grew bigger. Then Samuel laughed. His laughter made the floorboards shake.

Mother and Father told funny story after funny story. The twins forgot about the storm. Eliora's smile flashed through the clouds. A second later, Samuel's laugh boomed across the sky.

Finally, the storm ended. The rain stopped and the wind died down. Eliora and Samuel were not scared anymore.

The next time you are scared of lightning and thunder, think of Eliora and Samuel laughing at their parents' stories.

Eliora always smiles first. Then Samuel booms in with his laugh. That is why lightning always comes first, followed by thunder.

**Essential Questions** What sound does rain make? How do other kinds of weather sound the same or different?

# Weather

*by Eve Merriam*
*illustrated by Stephanie Dehennin*

Dot a dot dot dot a dot dot
Spotting the windowpane.

Spack a spack speck flick a flack fleck
Freckling the windowpane.

A spatter a scatter a wet cat a clatter
A splatter a rumble outside.

Umbrella umbrella umbrella umbrella
Bumbershoot barrel of rain.

Slosh a galosh slosh a galosh
Slither and slather a glide

A puddle a jump a puddle a jump
A puddle a jump puddle splosh

A juddle a pump a luddle a dump
A pudmuddle jump in and slide!

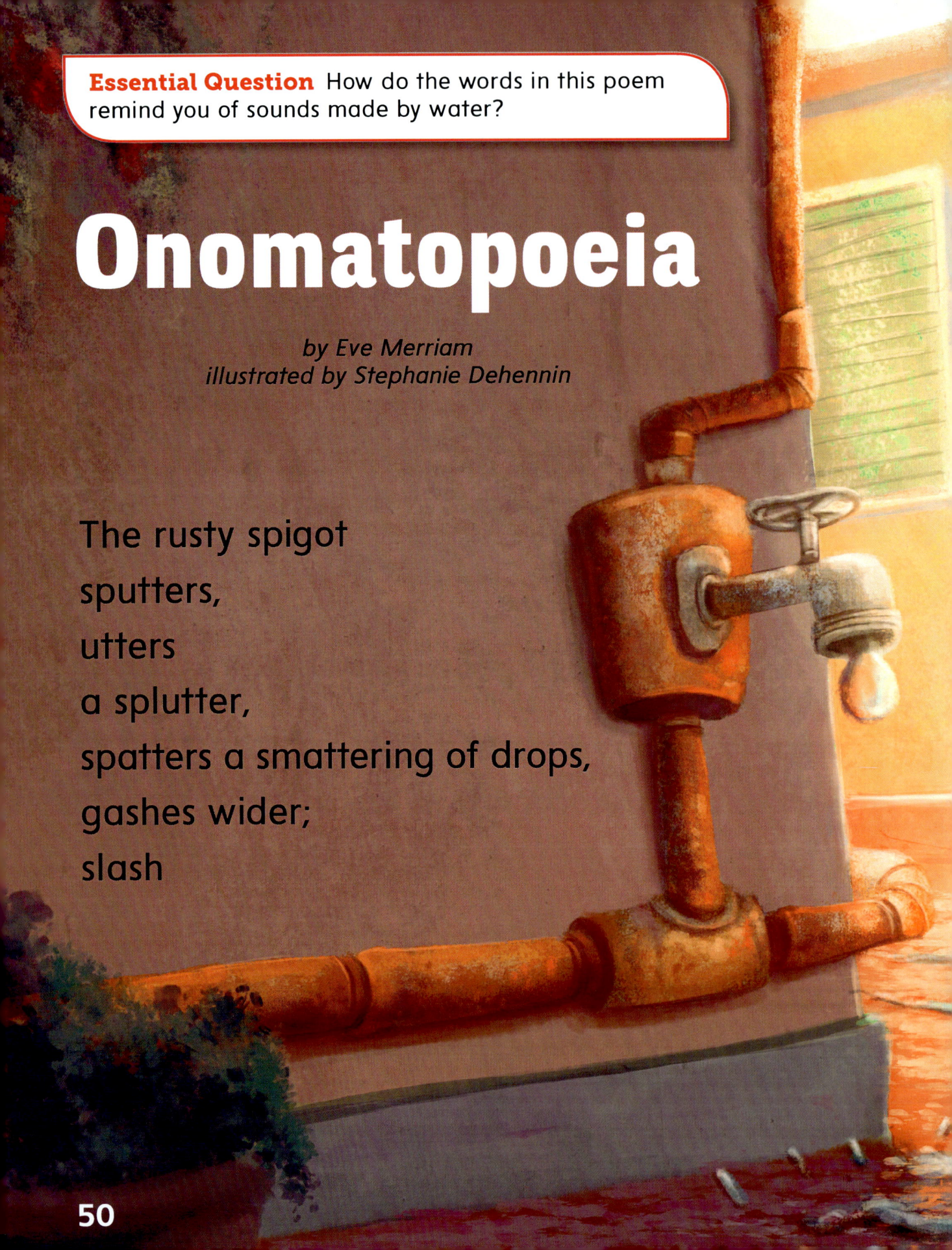

**Essential Question** How do the words in this poem remind you of sounds made by water?

# Onomatopoeia

by Eve Merriam
illustrated by Stephanie Dehennin

The rusty spigot
sputters,
utters
a splutter,
spatters a smattering of drops,
gashes wider;
slash

splatters
scatters
spurts
finally stops sputtering
and plash!
gushes rushes splashes
clear water dashes.

# Glossary

## B

**bounce**
to hit a surface and move in a different direction

## C

**contagious**
easily shared with others

## F

**forgot**
to not remember

## H

**however**
different from

## R

**ray**
one of the lines of light that you can see coming from an object

# S

**signals**
plural form of **signal**: a message

**sounds**
plural form of **sound**: something that is heard

# V

**vibrating**
to move back and forth or from side to side with very short, quick movements